Boy, Were We Wrong About the Weather!

Kathleen V. Kudlinski · illustrated by Sebastià Serra

DIAL BOOKS FOR YOUNG READERS · an imprint of Penguin Group (USA) LLC

DIAL BOOKS FOR YOUNG READERS
Published by the Penguin Group • Penguin Group (USA) LLC, 375 Hudson Street, New York, NY 10014

USA | Canada | UK | Ireland | Australia | New Zealand | India | South Africa | China
penguin.com

A PENGUIN RANDOM HOUSE COMPANY

Library of Congress Cataloging-in-Publication Data
Kudlinski, Kathleen V., author. • Boy, were we wrong about weather! / by Kathleen V. Kudlinski ; Illustrated by Sebastia Serra. • pages cm
Summary: "Examines what is known about weather—storms, predictions, climate, and other characteristics—and how different the facts are from what scientists, from ancient Sumerians to the recent past, believed to be true."— Provided by publisher.
Audience: Ages 3-5. • Audience: K to grade 3. • ISBN 978-0-8037-3793-8 (hardcover)
1. Weather forecasting—History—Juvenile literature. 2. Weather—Miscellanea—Juvenile literature. 3. Climatology—Miscellanea—Juvenile literature. I. Serra, Sebastià, 1966- illustrator. II. Title. • QC995.43.K83 2014   551.63—dc23   2014019185

Manufactured in China on acid free paper • 10 9 8 7 6 5 4 3 2 1

Designed by Jason Henry • Text set in Aptifer Slab • The artwork for this book was created with pencil and computer graphics.
The publisher does not have any control over and does not assume any
responsibility for author or third-party websites or their content.

For Henri, my son, with love
—K.V.K.

To nonno Julio, our own never-failing weatherman
—S.S.

Long, long ago, before people knew anything about the weather, even mighty Sumerian warriors were frightened by wild storms. They thought the weather god, Enlil, was angry. He was filling the sky with thunder and lightning.

The Sumerians did rain dances for Enlil, hoping to put him in a better mood. They believed that this would stop the storm and change the weather.

Boy, were they **wrong!**

Today we know that when warm moist air rises into the chilly upper atmosphere, a cloud of tiny water droplets forms. Some droplets cluster into raindrops and fall to earth. If strong winds blow these droplets up and down inside a cloud, it creates electricity. Excess electricity jumps out as lightning.

EVAPORATION

WATER CYCLE

RAIN

RUNOFF

THUNDERSTORM

Thunder is only the sound the lightning makes when it flashes.

We see lightning before we hear thunder because light travels faster than sound.

When explorers from Spain first crossed the Atlantic Ocean, they sailed into terrible storms. These storms were the worst they had ever seen. The fierce wind and rains sometimes sent whole ships to the bottom of the sea. The sailors that survived these storms later met the Taíno Indians. The Taínos explained that these storms were the work of their storm god, Huracan.

When the explorers came home, they told everyone about the "hurricane" storms. These stories sounded too bad to be true. People thought the explorers were making them up. **Boy,** were **they wrong!**

Now we know that hurricanes are real. They start out like thunderstorms. As they cross warm oceans, they become stronger and move faster, fueled by the warm water. They can grow to be five hundred miles wide with winds up to two hundred miles an hour.

Today, scientists warn people when a hurricane is heading their way so they can prepare for its arrival.

In ancient Greece, a wise man wrote a book called *Meteorologica*. In it he explained that everything in the world was a mix of earth, air, wind, and fire. Even the weather, he said, was caused by just these four elements.

Boy, was he **wrong!**

Now we know that the sun's heat has the biggest effect on the weather. The spin of the Earth sets huge winds swirling, blowing storms from one place to another. Every season, the Earth's tilt toward the sun changes the weather, too.

And there is still more.

Mountain ranges affect weather. So do glaciers and deserts, lakes and oceans. The heat and dust of big volcanoes change weather. So do huge cities and every mile of coastline. Weather is so complicated!

It takes today's supercomputers to keep track of all the facts we know and measurements we take. But even though the ancient wise man was wrong, we still use his old word "meteorology" to describe weather science.

People have never liked being surprised by the weather. So they searched for ways to predict it in advance. The ancient Chinese thought that if a dragonfly was seen flying up and down instead of sideways, it meant rain was coming. **Boy,** were they **wrong!**

But rain could be predicted in other ways. Over 2000 years ago, sailors on the high seas devised their own early warning system. *Red skies at morning, sailors take warning. Red skies at night, sailors' delight.* This actually worked because a morning sky that was red had a lot of water in it, meaning a storm was on the way. But a red sky at night meant the sunset contained a lot of dust, a sign of dry weather ahead.

Today, we have scientific instruments to help us predict the weather. A barometer measures air pressure. A change in the air pressure means there will be a change in the weather. Rising pressure is usually a sign of good weather to come. Falling pressure means that a storm is on the way.

We now know much more than the sailors of long ago. But we still make mistakes predicting weather. Meteorologists will not give up until they understand it all.

Long ago people thought our air and weather went all the way up to the stars. Boy, were they wrong! Today scientists send rockets filled with instruments to study the weather miles and miles above the Earth.

We now know that the higher you go, the thinner the air gets. Finally, it just completely disappears. Our planet is surrounded by a blanket of air. Beyond that is icy cold space.

We use to think that places with freezing weather year-round would never change. They would always have an icy climate. A hot, rainy climate would always grow a rain forest. It might rain in a desert, but overall its hot, dry climate never changes.

Boy, were we **wrong** about the **climate!**

Well, what do you know!

Scientists have found fossils from warm weather dinosaurs deep under the Arctic
ice. So the Arctic wasn't always cold. And proof of mile-thick glaciers have been found
under deserts or jungles. So that land wasn't always hot. The glaciers melted away
after the Ice Ages in Earth's past. Those climate changes happened by themselves
thousands and thousands of years ago.

But climate change can occur for other reasons, too. Scientists today are concerned about how people are affecting our weather. As the earth's population grows, we keep burning more fuel—coal, wood, gas, oil, and gasoline.

Burning fuels puts sooty dust into the air and releases a gas called carbon dioxide.

More than a hundred years ago, a Swedish scientist started wondering if all that extra soot and carbon dioxide would trap the heat of the sun inside our blanket of air. **Boy, was he right!**

Now we know that the whole Earth's temperature is rising. This is called global warming. But the Earth's giant swirling winds, oceans, and mountains are spreading the heat unevenly. Some places are cooling down while others are heating up.

There is flooding now where it never happened before. In some places, rain has almost stopped falling. Fierce heat waves and bitter cold snaps are becoming more common. And devastating storms that used to happen once a century are hitting far too often.

Weather satellites orbiting the Earth measure, record, and photograph these changes. Scientists are studying these new weather patterns. They know what used to happen before. By analyzing these new patterns, they hope to figure out what will happen next.

We can still slow global warming if we slow down our fuel-burning and tree-cutting ways. Solar and wind power can help lessen our dependence on fossil fuels. Some people still think global warming is a myth. **Boy**, are they **wrong!**

Scientists are still hard at work trying to understand the hows and whys of the weather. Some study germs that help raindrops form. Others try to predict the start of tornadoes or hurricanes. Some are even investigating strange weather on other planets. There is so much we still don't understand.

Maybe when you grow up, you could be one of the scientists who makes us all say, "Boy, were we **wrong** about the weather!"

Time Line for Weather Science

1500 B.C.	Hittites dance to weather god where Turkey is today.
c. **340** B.C.	The Greek philosopher Aristotle writes *Meteorologica* and explains that rain is evaporated from water on Earth.
1441	Prince Munjong of Korea invents a rain gauge.
1450	Leon Battista Alberti—the first anemometer to measure wind speed
1492	Spanish explorers sail into hurricane in the Atlantic Ocean.
1643	Evangelista Torricelli invents the barometer.
1648	Blaise Pascal says atmospheric pressure decreases with height.
1714	Daniel Gabriel Fahrenheit invents a mercury thermometer.
1896	Swedish scientist Svante Arrhenius states Greenhouse Effect.
1930s	Global warming trend since late nineteenth century reported
1960	The first successful weather satellite, TIROS-1, is launched.
1972	Ice cores show climate shifts in the past.
2005	Too many storms: National Hurricane Center runs out of names
2012	Superstorm Sandy floods parts of New York City for first time ever.

WEBSITES FOR MORE INFORMATION

National Atmospheric and Space Administration's Kids' Club: Videos and activities about satellites and more. http://www.nasa.gov/audience/forkids/kidsclub/flash/index.html

National Oceanic and Atmospheric Administration: Multimedia, explanations, and links for teachers (and students) on Climate Change and Weather. http://www.education.noaa.gov/Climate/ and http://www.education.noaa.gov/Weather_and_Atmosphere/